The Flow of Energy Through The Seasons

Producers

Decomposers   **Consumers**

Mark K. Crawford
Author

Amber Pickle
Illustrator

Today's Readers are Tomorrow's Leaders

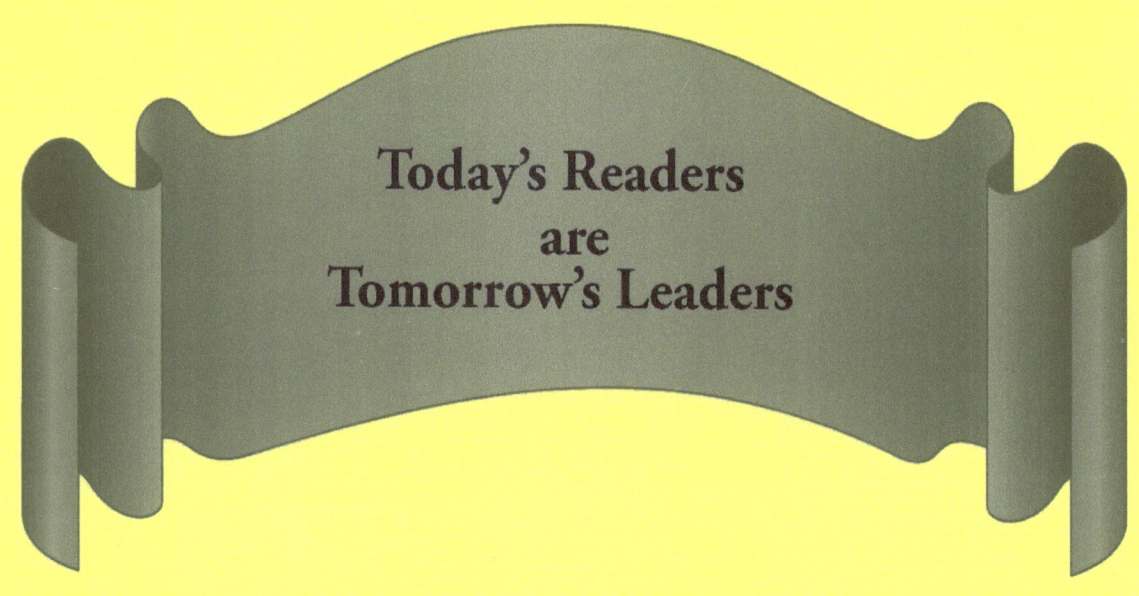

Mr. Crawford reading his first book, Beaver Ball, to his students.

Published By:

Vabella Publishing
PO Box 1052
Carrollton, Georgia 30112

Copyright © Mark K. Crawford 2024

All rights reserved. No part of this publication may be produced, stored in a retrieval system, or transmitted in any form by any means such as: electronic, mechanical, photocopying, recording, or otherwise, without prior permission from the author.

ISBN: 979-8-89450-002-7

Printed In The United States Of America

All Energy on Earth, comes from the Sun.

Last November, Mr. Crawford put the leaves that had fallen off the trees on top of his garden so they would begin to decompose and add rich nutrients to the soil.

The sun shone and the rains came. The snow fell on the leaves all winter long. This helped them decompose, adding rich nutrients to the garden's soil.

In the spring, Mr. Crawford planted tomato plants so they could produce juicy red tomatoes.

All through the spring and early summer, the tomato plants grew. The soil that was enriched with the nutrients from the decomposed leaves in Mr. Crawford's garden made them plump and juicy.

A Brown Thrasher bird pecked the juicy red tomatoes that got the rich nutrients from the decomposed leaves in Mr. Crawford's garden.

A long Black snake ate the Brown Thrasher bird that pecked the juicy red tomatoes that got the rich nutrients from the decomposed leaves in Mr. Crawford's garden.

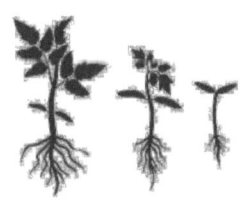

A Red-tailed hawk ate the long Black snake that ate the Brown Thrasher bird that pecked the juicy red tomatoes that got the rich nutrients from the decomposed leaves in Mr. Crawford's garden.

A Red fox ate the Red-tailed hawk that ate the long Black snake, that had eaten the Brown Thrasher bird, that pecked the juicy red tomatoes that got the rich nutrients from the decomposed leaves in Mr. Crawford's garden.

A Tan coyote ate the Red fox that ate the Red-tailed hawk, that had eaten the long Black snake, that ate the Brown Thrasher bird, that pecked the juicy red tomatoes that got the rich nutrients from the decomposed leaves in Mr. Crawford's garden.

A big Black panther ate the Tan coyote that ate the Red fox, that had eaten the Red-tailed hawk, that ate the long Black snake, that had eaten the Brown Thrasher bird, that pecked the juicy red tomatoes that got the rich nutrients from the decomposed leaves in Mr. Crawford's garden.

The big Black Panther went to the lake for a drink. He slipped on the muddy bank and fell in.

SPLASH!!! Oh No . . .

The big Black panther's body decomposed and added rich nutrients to the grass; a part of the ecosystem of the lake.

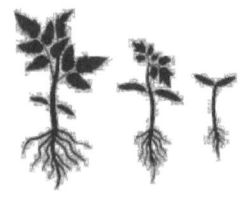

A lazy Blue catfish ate some of the grass growing in the lake. The grass had gotten rich nutrients that the decomposing body of the big Black panther had added to the ecosystem of the lake.

The next spring, Mr. Crawford went fishing. He caught the lazy Blue catfish that ate the lake's grass that had gotten the nutrients from the body of the big Black panther, who had eaten the Tan coyote, who ate the Red fox, who had eaten the Red-tailed hawk, who ate the long Black snake, who had eaten the Brown Thrasher bird who had pecked the juicy red tomatoes, that had gotten the rich nutrients from the decomposed leaves that Mr. Crawford had put in his garden last November.

Mr. Crawford is going to enjoy his fish dinner with his garden fresh tomatoes.

The flow of energy has completed its circle.

The End

Key Vocabulary Words

Brown Thrasher bird — State Bird of Georgia.

Consumer — A living creature the eats organisms from a different population.

Decomposer — An organism, especially a fungus or an invertebrate, that breaks down organic material.

Energy — The power that comes from physical or chemical resources, especially to provide light and heat.

Ecosystem — A biological community of interacting organisms and their physical environment.

Garden — A small piece of ground used to grow vegetables, fruits or flowers.

Nutrients — A substance that provides nourishment for growth and the maintenance of life.

Soil — The upper layer of earth in which plants grow.

Illustrator

Amber D. Pickle is an author, illustrator, and ghostwriter. She has edited, formatted for print, and created book designs and content to bring other authors' dreams to life for years.

Her ghostwriting works include "Healing Hearts," a novel, "Beyond the Bricks," based on true events surrounding the Liberian Civil War, and "Rise Up & Fly," a novel of personal and physical survival.

Her illustrated works include, "Where Do Puppies Come From?" and "Diggerydoo and Taller Too," a dinosaur story.

Mrs. Pickle has enjoyed every one of her projects, and working with Mr. Crawford was a particular joy.

She resides in Georgia with her husband and their many beloved pets.

Author

Mark Crawford has taught school for decades, as well as coaching baseball and football.

Mr. Crawford was born in a small town, and grew up in the rolling red clay hills of western Georgia. He loves poetry, literature, good music, and a tall tale.

He still resides in Georgia with his family, and currently presents living history skills and reading programs to school children.

Mr. Crawford brought Beaver Ball, his first book, to his audiences, young and old, with much anticipated pleasure and fun. He has yearned to put his stories to print for many of his teaching years. His next work is a nostalgic tale about a hundred-year-old bookstore.

www.ingramcontent.com/pod-product-compliance
Lightning Source LLC
LaVergne TN
LVHW072232080526
838199LV00116B/532